Billy the Kid

A Captivating Guide to a Notorious Gunfighter of the American Old West and His Feud with Pat Garrett

© Copyright 2021

All Rights Reserved. No part of this book may be reproduced in any form without permission in writing from the author. Reviewers may quote brief passages in reviews.

Disclaimer: No part of this publication may be reproduced or transmitted in any form or by any means, mechanical or electronic, including photocopying or recording, or by any information storage and retrieval system, or transmitted by email without permission in writing from the publisher.

While all attempts have been made to verify the information provided in this publication, neither the author nor the publisher assumes any responsibility for errors, omissions or contrary interpretations of the subject matter herein.

This book is for entertainment purposes only. The views expressed are those of the author alone, and should not be taken as expert instruction or commands. The reader is responsible for his or her own actions.

Adherence to all applicable laws and regulations, including international, federal, state and local laws governing professional licensing, business practices, advertising and all other aspects of doing business in the US, Canada, UK or any other jurisdiction is the sole responsibility of the purchaser or reader.

Neither the author nor the publisher assumes any responsibility or liability whatsoever on the behalf of the purchaser or reader of these materials. Any perceived slight of any individual or organization is purely unintentional.

Free Bonus from Captivating History (Available for a Limited time)

Hi History Lovers!

Now you have a chance to join our exclusive history list so you can get your first history ebook for free as well as discounts and a potential to get more history books for free! Simply visit the link below to join.

Captivatinghistory.com/ebook

Also, make sure to follow us on Facebook, Twitter and Youtube by searching for Captivating History.

Contents

INTRODUCTION 1
CHAPTER 1 – THE ORPHAN THIEF 3
CHAPTER 2 – FIRST BLOOD 12
CHAPTER 3 – THE LINCOLN COUNTY WAR 24
CHAPTER 4 – DYING YOUNG 36
CONCLUSION 46
HERE'S ANOTHER BOOK BY CAPTIVATING HISTORY THAT YOU MIGHT LIKE 47
FREE BONUS FROM CAPTIVATING HISTORY (AVAILABLE FOR A LIMITED TIME) 48
SOURCES 49

Introduction

Billy the Kid may have become one of the most legendary and deadly criminals of the Old West, but a life of crime was a path that he did not actively pursue at first. In fact, when he was still fourteen or fifteen years old, the Kid didn't choose crime. Crime chose him.

Many of us know Billy the Kid as a notorious outlaw, a legend of the Wild West. Indeed, sometimes it can be hard to separate fact from fiction when it comes to Billy the Kid. He himself claimed to have killed twenty-one men, "one for each year that I've been alive." In reality, he likely killed eight or nine, and only two of those were on his own. The rest died in shootings with other outlaws involved.

Nonetheless, the Kid was certainly a deadly criminal, yet looking into his life offers a glimpse into a tragic past. We all know that Billy the Kid was an Old West murderer, but did you know that he grew up in a New York City slum? Did you know that his deadbeat dad walked out on him right before his beloved mother died? Did you know that most of his murders followed the day that his mentor and friend, John Henry Tunstall, was killed in cold blood right in front of his eyes?

Billy the Kid is an emblem of a piece of history as problematic, complicated, and yet charismatic as he was: the American Old West. Just like the Wild West, the Kid has become legendary. And just like the West, he endured terrible suffering, made terrible choices, and bore the awful consequences.

And this is his story.

Chapter 1 – The Orphan Thief

Billy the Kid would ultimately become a legend of the Wild West, but he was born a nobody, a poor boy in some of the darkest slums in New York City.

Both of his parents—Catherine and Patrick McCarty—were from one of the most downtrodden and oppressed minorities across the globe during that era: the Irish. It was the 1850s, just a handful of years after Ireland had found itself in an indescribable crisis during the Great Potato Famine of 1845, which killed around one million Irish people. They fled in droves to England and to the New World, but wherever the Irish went, they were met with derision and hatred. The United States of America was no exception. This profoundly Protestant nation looked with great disfavor upon the Irish, who were mostly Catholic, and treated them as being less than human.

New York City was one of the most appalling places to live as an Irish person during the late 19th century. While the majority of the city was already a sprawling mass of poor tenement buildings, many Irish were denied access even to the moderately better tenements where living conditions were vaguely humane. Instead, they were crammed into the worst slums of the Lower East Side. Some accounts describe utterly chilling living conditions, almost unimaginable to most readers: single rooms housing as many as five families, with one or two families to a bed and no access to running water or any kind of basic sanitation, with corners of the same room where people slept and ate being used as lavatories. Filth upon filth piled up in these slums. There were few opportunities for the Irish, and in desperation, many turned to all kinds of crimes.

History is vague on the subject of Catherine and Patrick McCarty, but it would appear that Catherine, at least, was just a normal woman who was trying to eke out an honest living and a tolerable existence for herself and her family. There is very little information on her husband, Patrick, except that he fathered both of Catherine's children. The first was born on a disputed date in 1859, possibly September 28th. This was a little boy, whom she named Henry. It was Henry who would later become a scourge of the Old West. But at his birth, he was just another malnourished little baby, crying his nights away in the chaos of the Lower East Side.

Catherine's second child was born in 1863, and she named him Joseph McCarty, giving Henry a little brother. The little family of four continued trying to scratch out a living in their unsanitary home, but soon, things would change drastically.

Little Henry was somewhere between four and ten years old when he suffered the first of numerous awful losses that would pepper his short life. His father, Patrick, either died or left his family (sources differ) sometime during the 1860s. Catherine was left completely alone with two little boys and very few opportunities to make an honest living. As an Irish Catholic widow, she had almost no rights and practically no future. Still, she was determined to raise Henry and Joseph, and she held on to them fiercely. She decided to make a bold and radical move. She was going to move them from the slums of New York to find greener pastures in Indianapolis, Indiana, some seven hundred miles away.

How Catherine raised the funds for the journey and tackled it alone as a single woman with two very small boys, no one knows. In fact, we don't even know how old Henry was when his mother undertook the trip; he was younger than eleven at least, and little Joseph couldn't have been much more than a toddler. Indianapolis was not particularly welcoming to this Irish widow with her two little boys, but Catherine did find one piece of solace: William Henry Harrison Antrim.

As with much of Henry's early life, very little is known about what William was really like as a man and as Catherine's boyfriend, but he would certainly prove to be a disreputable character later in Henry's life. But for a time, Catherine seemed to be in love with him, and she soon began a steady relationship with him.

By 1870, Catherine and William were living together, and they decided to leave Indiana behind and embark on a journey that would take them even farther west and into a region that had recently been torn apart by the American Civil War: Kansas. With the boys in tow, Catherine and William arrived in Wichita, Kansas, another seven hundred miles from Indianapolis, sometime in 1870. Henry was around eleven years old by then, and little Joseph was seven, and they were about to step into what might have been the only happy period of Henry McCarty's life.

Wichita was good to Catherine and the rest of her little family. It's unclear what William did to occupy his time, but Catherine proved to be a hardworking and resourceful woman, certainly one not content with simply sitting back and allowing destiny to do to her as it would. She had an entrepreneurial spirit and started several small businesses in town, including laundry services and working in property sales. Irish or not, Catholic or not, female or not, Catherine was not going to let anything get in the way of her future with her children and William.

Henry and Joseph likely spent their days like any other kid in Wichita. They went to school, where Henry proved to be a good, quiet, courteous, and charming little student who loved to read. In the afternoons, they would play with their friends all over town, little Joseph forever tagging along as Henry and the big boys played cowboys and Indians or cops and robbers. Little did young Henry know then that his childhood games of cat and mouse eventually would bleed into his real life with real-life stakes.

For now, though, Henry enjoyed long, happy days of playing with his friends and brother, days of just being a normal kid. For three years, the boy who would become Billy the Kid was able to actually be a kid. But trouble loomed on the horizon. Trouble that would ultimately lead to a bloodthirsty life of crime.

* * * *

Henry was fourteen years old when Catherine's doctor gave her some absolutely devastating news: she had consumption.

Catherine had achieved more in her life than most American women could dream of at the time. She'd taken her children from a New York slum to a carefree life in a Western boomtown. She owned businesses and made her own way in the world instead of waiting for a man to do it for her. And now her doctor was telling her that she didn't have much time left to live.

Consumption was, back then, a death knell for thousands of people all over the world. It was a vivid description of a disease that seemed to eat its victims alive, known today as tuberculosis. While tuberculosis is nearly unheard-of in developed countries today, and its incidence across the globe continues to fall steadily, it is still a deadly illness that preys upon the immunocompromised.

In 1873, however, tuberculosis was still a global threat and a silent killer that stalked all humanity. This was before antibiotics or even a thorough understanding of modern disease theories, and so, people with tuberculosis almost invariably died. For Catherine, it must have been like a diagnosis of cancer.

The doctor's recommendation was a common one for the time: to move south, away from the ravaging winters that would make Catherine's fragile lungs even more vulnerable. And so, with William and the boys in tow, Catherine was forced to leave the one place where she had been truly happy.

Teenage Henry must have felt that his whole world was about to change. His blissful existence in Wichita with his academics, his books, his friends, and his brother was being stripped away from him, and the next thing he knew, his mother was moving them six hundred miles south to Santa Fe, New Mexico. Another major change took place shortly after they arrived in Santa Fe. Catherine and William had been together for a minimum of four years or so by this point yet had never married. But spurred on by the hovering specter of her own death—and possibly trying to secure a future for Henry and Joseph after she was gone—Catherine decided it was time that they were officially married. The ceremony was performed in a church in Santa Fe, and fourteen-year-old Henry and ten-year-old Joseph were the witnesses for the marriage.

Henry's life had gotten suddenly very complicated. While little is known about his relationship with William at that point, Henry must have had a little trouble accepting that William was now officially his stepfather. It would be an adjustment for any child, let alone a child whose mother had been given a devastating diagnosis and who had just moved across the country from his friends. Nonetheless, both Henry and Joseph would take William Antrim's last name, and Henry McCarty became Henry Antrim.

Their stay in Santa Fe didn't last long. Soon, William and Catherine moved their little family three hundred miles south to Silver City, New Mexico. This new environment would soon prove instrumental in shaping the person that young Henry was to become. Silver City was a town in its infancy, having existed for only around three years when the Antrim family moved there; much of it still consisted of tents instead of buildings. As the name indicated, it had exploded into existence after silver was discovered in the nearby landscape, with prospectors flooding into the town. It was silver that had brought the Antrims there too. The journey from Wichita had sapped all but the very last of Catherine's strength, and the bustling, resourceful, industrious mother that Henry had once known was reduced to a pale skeleton of her former self. She was unable to work, and so, perhaps for the first time, William became the sole breadwinner. Prospecting was the only way he could think of to earn a living.

Silver was abundant in Silver City, but it also came at a high price. The Apache tribe still controlled large tracts of New Mexico, and they weren't about to surrender their ancestral lands to the influx of white settlers without a fight. In fact, the founder of Silver City himself had been killed just a year after the town was built, dying in an Apache raid. The threat of attack hung heavy over the town, and while it's hard to blame the Apache for defending their home, their ominous presence must have had an effect on Henry.

More than that, Silver City was completely lawless at the time. The hundreds of miners living there were not governed by any sheriff, and crime was rampant as poverty rose. For every prospector who succeeded in finding silver, there were many who were reduced to starving beggars.

This was a fate that would soon face the Antrim family. Catherine had always been the heart and soul of the family and the only reason for its continued financial survival. Now that she was bedridden, William completely failed to pick up the slack. They had moved to

Silver City so that he could work in the mines; instead, William mostly gambled, losing more than he won, as gamblers often do. Henry and Joseph went from having a happy, carefree childhood, with friends and playtime and an education, to being two hungry children with a dying mother. The sicker Catherine became, the more William withdrew into himself and his gambling. It seems the thought of losing her was more than he could even imagine.

By 1874, Catherine's condition was critical. Fifteen-year-old Henry and eleven-year-old Joseph were faced with the terrible prospect of losing the woman who had been their anchor and pillar all their lives, but before they would be dealt that devastating blow, another tragedy quickly befell them. If Catherine had married William in the hopes that he would care for the boys when she died, she had overestimated William's commitment to their marriage and family. With Catherine on her deathbed, instead of supporting the boys, William simply left, disappearing from Silver City and from the lives of the boys.

Henry was left with a dying mother and with a little brother who could now only look to Henry for help and safety. The responsibility must have been crushing; the fear, even more so. It is unknown how Henry and Joseph survived for the next few months, but it must have been terrifying.

Tuberculosis was doing exactly what it always did: it was consuming Catherine, piece by piece. Her toiling lungs grew less and less capable of sustaining her body as she was reduced to little more than a skeleton wrapped in blue-tinged skin. There was nothing anyone could do for her, not in the 1870s. Slowly, agonizingly, she continued to fade in front of Henry's eyes as he struggled to care for his mother and little brother all on his own. She breathed her last on September 16th, 1874.

Catherine's death was a terrible trauma and must have plunged the boys into inexpressible grief, but Henry didn't have time to grieve; there were even more pressing concerns in his life. His parents were dead, his stepfather had disappeared, and he had a little brother to care for. Silver City was no place for an orphan, and Henry and Joseph may very well have faced an uncertain fate—and Billy the Kid may have lived an even shorter life—if it weren't for a few kind families in the city who decided to take them in. The boys were separated, and Henry found himself completely alone and dependent on the kindness of strangers.

For whatever reason, Henry never managed to stay with any of his foster homes for very long. Perhaps most families simply didn't have the resources to feed another mouth long-term; perhaps grief and anger had made Henry difficult to deal with, although most accounts suggest that Catherine's death did not change him on the surface and that he was still the sweet, funny, polite boy he had been back in Wichita.

Either way, by 1875, the troubled youngster was considered old enough to earn his keep, if not any wages. He was sent to live and work in the Star Hotel in Silver City, owned and managed by one Sarah Brown. He was something of a general worker, washing dishes and waiting on guests. It is unclear whether Henry was paid anything at all for his work, even though he was fast approaching sixteen, but he was given a roof over his head and presumably some food. Clearly, however, Henry's circumstances were not ideal. Perhaps Brown was abusive, as so many people were of their employees in those days. Beatings may have become a part of Henry's life; he was fed barely enough to survive, and so, Henry began to grow more and more desperate.

Every bit of stability that Henry had ever known was gone. He was fending for himself now, and he knew he had to do whatever it took to survive. Soon, he would be faced with a choice that would send him down a slippery slope to a violent life and an early death.

That choice had to do, prosaically, with butter. In the Star Hotel's dealings, plenty of merchandise came through the doors, and one day, Henry found himself alone with several pounds of a rancher's fresh butter. It was a fairly expensive and luxurious commodity in Silver

City at the time, and Henry knew he could capitalize on it. He stole the butter, sold it quickly to another merchant, and finally had some money for the first time since his mother had died.

But the boy was not yet the seasoned criminal that he would later become. It wasn't long before Sarah Brown found out what he had done, and she was quick to call for Silver City's brand-new sheriff, Harvey Whitehill. Sheriff Whitehill was a formidable figure in his late thirties; a veteran of the Apache Wars, Whitehill had been chosen to bring order to the wilderness of Silver City for a reason, and Henry must have been terrified when he found out that Sheriff Whitehill was going to handle his case.

The moment that Sheriff Whitehill set eyes on Henry, however, he knew that this was no hardened criminal. Henry had always been a small, skinny boy with youthful features and great, sad, brilliantly blue eyes, and he looked more pitiful than ever now, a ragged little orphan who was completely alone in the world. Sheriff Whitehill couldn't bring himself to punish the boy. He simply gave Henry a stern talking-to and allowed him to return to the Star Hotel and continue with his life in peace.

Perhaps this reprieve would have convinced some boys to stay forever on the right side of the law after that. But Henry's encounter with Sheriff Whitehill seemed to have exactly the opposite effect.

It wouldn't be long before the sheriff would have no choice but to clap young Henry in irons.

Chapter 2 – First Blood

Illustration I: A photograph of Billy the Kid by Ben Wittick

After the theft of the butter and his encounter with Sheriff Whitehill, young Henry continued to live and work in the Star Hotel, but his life was by no means easy. Apart from the hard work and the lack of good food, Henry was also deeply deprived of something he constantly missed: a family. William had been imperfect, and like all siblings, Henry and Joseph must have squabbled. Even Catherine could hardly have been all sunshine and roses. But all his life, even in the ugly slums of New York, even through the many moves across the country, Henry had had the stability of a family unit.

Now even that was gone. And having been in Silver City for only about two years, most of those years spent caring for his bedridden mother and little Joseph or bouncing around foster homes, Henry didn't have many friends at all.

The only person he counted as being a friend was a man named George Schaefer, also known as Sombrero Jack. Like a vast number of the men in Silver City at the time, Jack was bad news. He drank constantly and gambled even more so, possibly even in the hotel, if Sarah Brown was in the habit of serving drinks to anyone who would pay for them. Whether Henry knew it or not, Jack was also a thief. But perhaps it didn't matter to Henry even if he did know since Jack was the only person in his world who treated him with kindness.

It's unclear what Jack's motivations really were for being the only kind face that Henry ever saw. Perhaps Jack's heart was touched by the plight of this sweet young orphan, with his gentle voice and big, mournful eyes. Given how this part of Henry's story ends, however, it's far more likely that Jack knew an opportunity when he saw it. Jack more than likely knew that Henry would be an easy target, someone easy to manipulate and easy to use whenever and however he saw fit.

One day in 1875, Jack knew it was time to use his young friend for his intended purpose. He had just robbed the laundry down the street, which, like most laundries of the time, was staffed almost entirely by overworked Chinese men. Jack had stolen a large bundle of clothes from the laundry, as well as two guns, and he needed somewhere to hide it. With Sheriff Whitehill rapidly cleaning up Silver City, Jack was running out of hiding spaces.

He went over to the Star Hotel and got the attention of young Henry. Pointing out to Henry that he was wearing little more than rags, Jack offered him the bundle of clothes. It would appear that Henry was aware that the clothes had been stolen. Nonetheless, the boy was desperate. He took the bundle and hurried to hide it in his room, where Mrs. Brown discovered it in a trunk a short while later. She knew immediately that the clothes had been stolen.

Once again, Mrs. Brown was quick to call on Sheriff Whitehill, and this time, the sheriff knew that his stern talking-to had had no effect on Henry's choices when it came to crime. He decided that he was going to scare the boy straight, and he arrested him and dragged him to the Silver City jailhouse.

Henry would be held for a short while before he would be required to appear in court. It seems, however, that Sheriff Whitehill was not particularly interested in prosecuting the boy. He just wanted to make it clear that a life of crime would not be tolerated in Silver City and to hopefully influence Henry to make better choices. Accordingly, Sheriff Whitehill didn't leave young Henry locked up in the cells with the real criminals. Instead, he let him stay in the hallway outside the cells, giving him a little more freedom to move about. By all accounts, Sheriff Whitehill treated Henry with respect, trying to be kind to him. Perhaps, if Henry had only reached out, if he had only seen that Sheriff Whitehill's tough love held far more kindness than Sombrero Jack's empty promises and smooth words, his life might have been a very different one.

But Henry saw Sheriff Whitehill as the enemy; the star on his chest made him evil in Henry's eyes, and while he was civil and courteous to the sheriff the way he was to everyone at that point in his life, Henry knew he had to escape. He was locked in the hallway; Sheriff Whitehill knew that Henry wasn't a seasoned enough criminal to pick a lock. But the sheriff had underestimated Henry's slenderness and agility. His thin frame had often been the subject of ridicule by other boys, but now, it was his ticket to freedom. After just two days in custody, Henry climbed into the fireplace, reached into the chimney, and shimmied right out onto the jailhouse roof. From there, it was just a hop, a skip, and a jump to freedom.

The moment Henry's feet hit the ground outside the jailhouse, he knew immediately that his life had changed. He had been abused, starved, and overworked before; he had always been just an orphan, just a kid. Suddenly, although the moniker of "the Kid" would follow him for the rest of his brief years, Henry had to start thinking like a man. Child or not, he was an escapee now. He was a fugitive from the law.

Mrs. Brown was his erstwhile guardian, but she had proven twice that she couldn't be trusted in Henry's eyes by turning him in to the sheriff. Sombrero Jack had betrayed him and had since disappeared completely from Silver City. Now, Henry turned to the only people he could think of, a couple named the Truesdells, who lived nearby and had been among the people to foster him after his mother died. They were horrified when Henry turned up at their door. A story had been printed in the *Grant County Herald* shortly before Henry's escape, and while its wording was generally sympathetic to Henry, calling him "the tool of Sombrero Jack," it had made it clear that Henry had been arrested. The Truesdells knew at once that Henry was a fugitive from the law.

However, instead of turning him in to face the wrath of Sheriff Whitehill, they decided that it was high time his stepfather stepped up to the plate. They knew that William Antrim had gone to Clifton, Arizona, ostensibly for prospecting (although it would appear that William did about as much prospecting in Clifton as he did in Silver City). So, they bought a ticket and loaded the young Henry on a stagecoach to Clifton, hoping that William would be able to get some sense into him.

The stagecoach journey must have been a frightening one for Henry. Given all the traveling that he had done with his family in earlier years, he must have traveled by stagecoach before but never alone. Now, he found himself being jostled from one stage to the other, always swapping drivers, switching passengers, surrounded by strangers. He had just run from the law, and every other person he saw must have looked like a sheriff to him.

It was a wide-eyed and scared teenager who found himself on the doorstep of his stepfather's home in Clifton. Henry was frightened and desperate, and at first glance, William must have been able to tell how much hardship the boy had endured since William had walked out on him. He was clothed in rags, half-starved, and filthy, the kind of condition that Catherine would never have allowed.

If Henry had hoped that the sight of him would inspire some kind of paternal warmth in his stepfather, his hopes were entirely in vain. William allowed him to come inside and stay with him, but his stay was very brief—perhaps only a few days. It would appear that William was still mostly interested in gambling and generally being a deadbeat, but he was very quick to judge Henry based on the boy's own mistakes.

It didn't take long for William to pry the truth out of Henry about what had happened back in Silver City. As soon as William heard that Henry had been arrested for theft, he lost his temper, telling him that he was unworthy of staying in his house and ordering him to get out. The moment William's back was turned, Henry did just that but not before helping himself to some of William's supplies.

It had been made abundantly obvious to Henry that he had absolutely no one left in the world. His little brother Joseph had been passed on to a foster family back in New Mexico, nearly a hundred miles away, an impassable distance for a lonely boy on foot. Besides, his foster families hadn't wanted him, Mrs. Brown had betrayed him, and even Sombrero Jack had chosen to use him and then disappear. Perhaps, ironically, the only person left in Silver City who might have helped him was the sheriff. But in Henry's eyes, Sheriff Whitehall was his greatest enemy.

He was on his own. And his youthful heart, hopelessly scarred by the grief, abuse, desperation, and lack he had endured, had grown hard and cold. He thought nothing of taking clothes from William's closet and helping himself to some of William's supply of guns before walking out into the wilderness of Arizona.

* * * *

It was a very different person who left William Antrim's home for good. Henry was no longer the wide-eyed innocent who had been a teacher's pet that liked to read. Hardship had toughened him, and despite the fact that his cheeks were still smooth and his frame still puny, Henry felt that he was a little boy no longer. In conduct, he thought himself a man.

The truth was, as he headed southeast deeper into the Territory of Arizona, Henry was still just fifteen or sixteen years old. But he had no choice. All the people he depended on had failed him. He could only trust himself now.

It was this hardened youth who found a job working as a ranch hand in Arizona. Though his wages couldn't have been much, they were all his, and it was better than living with Sarah Brown. Still, Henry had no idea what to really do with money, and he was surrounded by the rough cowboys of the Wild West. They were bad influences on him, and he turned to gambling just like his stepfather, squandering his wages at the poker table. His job at that ranch didn't last very long, but his career as a ranch hand continued in 1876 when he went to work for businessman and rancher Henry Hooker. Hooker was a skilled businessman and an upright citizen—in fact, he was a friend of one of the Old West's most famous lawmen, Wyatt Earp. He was also the employer of one of its most infamous criminals—Billy the Kid.

Having grown rich on a single wild scheme involving herding five hundred turkeys over the Sierra River, Hooker now owned a prosperous ranch called Sierra Bonita, and it was here that young Henry Antrim worked. Perhaps Hooker could have taught Henry a thing or two, but instead, Henry was attracted to another man who tended to hang around the ranch: John R. Mackie. Mackie was about as disreputable as one could get. The Scotsman had been in the US Army in past years, but war had made him harsh and bitter, and the bloody realities of what he had witnessed had failed to build in his spirit the kind of loyal camaraderie that they inspired in so many other soldiers. Instead, Mackie cared only for himself.

He had been stationed at Camp Grant, a fort near the Sierra Bonita Ranch, and he still tended to hang around the outskirts of the army camp. His intentions, however, were by no means sentimental or nostalgic. Camp Grant was filled with cavalrymen and their fast, fit horses. In Arizona Territory at the time, horses were not simply a means of transport; they were a means of survival. A man on horseback could cross hundreds of miles of desert, whereas a man on foot would starve. Horses made it possible to transport goods, flee from enemies, and survive. And, of course, they were priced accordingly.

While horse theft carried a heavy penalty—hanging—it was still a business in which many criminals were interested thanks to its lucrative nature. John R. Mackie was no exception. Stealing horses from the US Army was so much easier than actually serving in it. It wasn't long before he introduced Henry to this lucrative business, and the two men started stealing and smuggling horses out of Camp Grant regularly.

It was around this time in 1877, as Henry's notoriety began to grow, that he needed an alias, which was a common practice in the Old West. Back then, the West was populated by people with nicknames like Wild Bill, Crazy Steve, and Calamity Jane. For Henry, it was easy to choose one. Among the grizzled veterans of the criminal world surrounding him, he stood out like a sore thumb: a scrawny, weak-jawed figure, with not even a trace of a beard, his youthfulness obvious in every line of his face and body. It wasn't long before he was becoming known as "Kid Antrim" or just "the Kid," a nickname that would stay with him for the few years he had left to live.

In a matter of two years, the Kid had escalated from getting a sheriff's scolding for stealing some butter to committing a capital crime by stealing horses from an Army camp. And it wasn't long before he sank even deeper into crime. He was taking horses now, but soon, he would take a human life.

* * * *

After his stint working as a ranch hand for Henry Hooker, Kid Antrim found a new job closer to the scene of most of his crimes. In fact, this new position was right in the middle of Camp Grant, and it even led him to work with the very animals he was stealing from the army camp.

Stealing so many horses had given the Kid a way with them, and he proved himself to be a capable horseman. Along with his youth and agility, this made him an ideal candidate to work as a teamster. His task was to hitch two enormous draft horses to logs that had been hewed in the woods just down the hill from Camp Grant and then juggle the horses and the log as the mighty animals hauled it up the hill. It was a tricky task, but the Kid took to it well, and it made it even easier for him and Mackie to steal horses.

In his role, the Kid would encounter a man who became a terrible thorn in his side. This was Frank Cahill, nicknamed Windy. Windy was a blacksmith, and he and the Kid met each other often as he trimmed and shod the draft horses' feet. What was more, they both frequented the same saloon in the nearby village of Bonita. Windy was a huge, angry, sharp-tongued figure who instantly resented the Kid's popularity. Despite the fact that he was now a seasoned thief, the Kid was still the same nice young man whose teachers had liked him back in Wichita and Silver City. Everyone liked him. Everyone but Windy.

Whenever the Kid was in the saloon, he just wanted to relax. It was the place where all the men gathered, and while the Kid was still a few weeks from his eighteenth birthday, he had long since stopped thinking of himself as a boy. He just wanted to drink, gamble, and hang out in peace. But Windy made that impossible. He loved to sling insults at the Kid after a few drinks, and sometimes, it went further than just insults. It started when he would simply ruffle the Kid's unruly dark hair, but soon, he started to shove him around, shouting and spitting in his face, pushing him to the floor. And most of the time, the Kid was his usual polite self, never allowing the confrontation to escalate—until one fateful evening.

August 17th, 1877, was the day that the Kid's life changed forever. He wasn't looking for trouble at the time. Why would he? He had a lucrative criminal career and plenty of friends; all he wanted to do was spend some of his stolen earnings on booze. But when Windy shouted at him as usual, calling him a "pimp," something snapped inside the Kid. He wheeled around and shouted at Windy that he was a "son of a b***."

Windy let out a roar of anger and lunged across the saloon. Like any blacksmith, he was a massive, powerful, heavily built man, easily twice the weight of the Kid, and he was an imposing figure as he attacked. The Kid was thrown to the ground, and Windy was on top, straddling the Kid's thin body. Blows rained down on the Kid's face as Windy's meaty fists pounded into his delicate features.

The Kid panicked. But instead of waiting for his friends to come to his aid, he reached for the pistol that always rested in his holster. He had never yet used it to draw human blood, but tonight, all that would change. He wrestled it out of the holster. It's unclear whether he actually meant to pull the trigger, but either way, there was a terrible, deafening crack, and blood bloomed across Windy's abdomen. The blacksmith collapsed, and the panicking Kid slithered out from under him. His clothes were stained with Windy's blood.

Windy was still breathing, but the blood was spreading in a massive pool around the fallen blacksmith. The Kid knew that Windy wouldn't survive and that he had just killed a man in the middle of a crowded saloon. Panic seized him, and he rushed out of the building. The patrons' horses were standing tied outside, and his eyes rested immediately on a long-limbed animal with strong muscles and wide nostrils—a racehorse. The Kid yanked its reins free, vaulted into the saddle, and spurred it away into the desert.

The swift horse carried the Kid away into the night but not away from the reality of what he had done or the fact that he had no idea what he was going to do next. He hid in the desert for a few days, long enough that he realized that there were countless angry Apache out there and that there was little water or food. He couldn't survive, he had no one to turn to, and he didn't know what to do. So, he returned to Camp Grant, which was a terrible mistake.

After the Kid had fled from the area, Windy died, bleeding out painfully and slowly through the bullet hole in his abdomen. The justice of the peace in the area— Miles Wood—was out for blood: the Kid's blood. It seems that once again, the Kid's friends had all abandoned him. He was arrested a few days after Windy's death, and Wood took him to the Camp Grant guardhouse, where he could be kept under lock and key until the sheriff could come and take him away.

The Kid was terrified. He knew that this time, he was facing a far greater threat than Sheriff Whitehill and his tough love. It had already been decided that the shooting was unjustifiable. The Kid had committed murder, and he knew he would hang for it. His only hope of survival was to escape. And escaping from Camp Grant would be far harder than shimmying up the chimney of the jailhouse in Silver City, for this time, the Kid had been placed in iron shackles and was kept inside a real cell.

The Kid was in luck, however. There was a dance going on in the nearby village that evening, and the guards believed that the Kid wasn't going anywhere, seeing as he was shackled and behind bars. They went off to attend the dance, and when they returned, the cell and the shackles were empty. It's not clear how he did it, but Kid Antrim had escaped again.

Once again, the Kid stole a horse and rode off into the night, but this time, he knew there could be no going back to his cushy life in Camp Grant. Instead, he decided that he would have to flee right across territorial lines. He only knew the way to one place: Silver City. It was the only place he could think of to go. Alone and in darkness, the Kid rode toward New Mexico as fast as his horse could carry him.

But traveling alone was a terrifying and dangerous undertaking, even for a murderer. The Kid was armed, but he was also heavily outnumbered when a band of Apache attacked. It's not clear whether the Apache saw him as an enemy or simply as an opportunity. Possibly, they were just raiders or thieves because they could have easily killed the Kid if they so chose. Instead, they simply threw him to the ground, stole his horse, and disappeared into the desert.

The Kid now found himself in as much mortal peril as he had been back in that guardhouse. Alone in the desert, with no food, no water, no horse, and no weapons, he was a dead man walking. If predators or Apache didn't kill him, starvation or thirst certainly would. But there was no turning back now. All he could do was continue stumbling onward through the desert, with its jagged red peaks and its endless sagebrush, and hope that he would eventually find his way home.

The Kid didn't quite make it to Silver City, but he did find his way to an old friend: an outlaw named John Jones. Jones lived in Dona Ana County, New Mexico, and somehow, the Kid dragged himself half-dead to Jones's door. He had trekked two hundred miles across the desert with practically no resources, and it was astonishing that he was alive at all. He was starving, his always-bony frame reduced to a pale skeleton, his great blue eyes filled with suffering. There was hardly any strength left in him, and he was at the brink of collapse when he met John Jones.

Jones quickly scooped up his young friend and carried him to his mother's home. It's unclear whether Barbara Jones was particularly supportive of her son's illegal endeavors, but even though the Kid was a murderer and a fugitive, she couldn't just let him die. Painstakingly, Barbara nursed him back to life, proving to be one of the Kid's few allies who was actually there for him when he needed it.

As soon as the Kid was well again, he knew he had to move on. He was a wanted man now, and not just for the theft of some clothes or horses but for killing Frank Cahill. Still, he was closer to Silver City than he had been in years, and he couldn't resist the pull of home. He rode to Silver City and visited there for a short while, spending time with some of the foster families that had taken him in after Catherine's death, including the Truesdells, who had first put him on that stagecoach to Arizona.

Still, the Kid couldn't stay long. Even though it felt like decades, it had been just three years since he'd fled Silver City, and he would be easily recognized. He began to wander across New Mexico, ultimately finding himself near Apache Tejo, a tiny settlement in Lincoln County.

There, the Kid accepted that ordinary work would never again be his lot in life. Instead, he joined a gang known simply as "the Boys," where his skill in stealing horses could be put to good use. The Boys were cattle rustlers, and Lincoln County was rich in abundant herds just ripe for the picking.

Little did the Kid know that some of those herds belonged to a man whose death would trigger one of the bloodiest feuds in the Old West. A feud that would catapult the Kid's name from notorious thief to enduring legend.

Chapter 3 – The Lincoln County War

Illustration II: John Henry Tunstall photographed in 1872

During his stint as a cattle rustler, the Kid continually grew in notoriety among his peers. Something about his sweet manners, innocent appearance, and deadly reputation quickly made him the stuff of legend, and rumors about him began to spread. It was perhaps because of this that the Kid finally stopped using his real name of Henry Antrim. Even "Kid Antrim" was no longer safe. Instead, he adopted an entirely new moniker: William Henry Bonney. It is possibly ironic that he chose to use his stepfather's first names, considering that William's abandonment was the event that had set Henry's life on this tragic trajectory in the first place. Either way, it wasn't long before he never heard the name Henry anymore, as he went by Billy instead. Thus was born one of the most famous aliases ever heard in the Old West: Billy the Kid.

* * * *

While Billy the Kid was growing in notoriety as a cattle rustler in Lincoln County, he was only a very small part of John Henry Tunstall's problems.

John Henry had been born in England, a young man from a wealthy middle-class family who had excellent prospects and was an eligible bachelor for many a twittering young Victorian-era socialite. All of this disgusted him. John Henry was hungry for one thing alone—adventure—and marriage did not fit into his plans. He moved to British Columbia, Canada, in the early 1870s to join his father's business (a general store in the town of Victoria). Canada was still a few years away from becoming a British colony, and it all felt terribly tame to John Henry. There were still girls who wanted to marry him and boring, ordinary business to conduct. He wanted more, and when a friend tried to persuade him to take up sheep ranching in California, John Henry was all too quick to accept.

He moved in February 1876, but ranching there quickly proved to be unsuccessful. Still, California had proved one thing to John Henry: the West was the place that he wanted to be. It was a wild area, filled with crime and danger, steeped in vice, but for a young man seeking adventure, there was no better place to be. John Henry moved to Lincoln County, New Mexico, in 1876.

By the time Billy the Kid arrived in Lincoln County, John Henry had finally found success, not only as an adventurer but also, finally, as a businessman. He owned a general store in the town of Lincoln itself, and his vast herds of horses and cattle roamed contentedly across the slopes of his nearby ranch. They were beautiful, fat, healthy animals—exactly the kind that the Boys loved to steal.

Deep in the winter of 1877, the Kid did what he could do best: he stole a handful of John Henry's horses. The rancher was outraged, and the sheriff was called in. He arrested the Kid quickly, charging him with theft. Instead of having the young man hanged, however, John Henry seemed to recognize a kindred spirit in young Billy's eyes. He was only six years older than Billy, and the young man's charming personality quickly won him over. Instead of pressing charges, John Henry gave the Kid a job as a cowboy and gunman on his ranch.

What the Kid might not have known was that his theft of John Henry's horses wasn't simply a crime of opportunity. In fact, the Boys, led by toughened outlaw Jesse Evans, had possibly been contracted to rustle John Henry's stock. This was all thanks to a deeply rooted feud that was being waged all over Lincoln County.

Before John Henry had come to Lincoln and gone into business with attorney Alexander McSween, two Irish-born businessmen had had almost complete control over the county's economy. These men were Lawrence Murphy and his protégé, James Dolan. Dolan, himself a veteran of the American Civil War, had had a harsh life until Murphy took him under his wing. Murphy was a visionary businessman, and he capitalized on every opportunity until his general store, the House, had a monopoly on the beef business in Lincoln. He made Dolan his business partner, which led to an easy and wealthy existence for Dolan until John Henry Tunstall showed up.

John Henry discovered that the House had made it nearly impossible for other cattle businesses to survive in Lincoln, and he decided that it was unjust for one business to control everything. He decided to set up a rival business, knowing that many cattle ranchers were unhappy with the state of affairs and hoping to make a fortune for himself.

By this time, Lawrence Murphy was lying in a hospital in Lincoln, sick and dying from cancer. Dolan was already losing the man who served as a father figure for him, and now, he was in danger of losing his very business to this young upstart. To make matters worse, enmity still simmered between the Irish and English everywhere. Dolan started to grow angrier as John Henry's business continued to grow. He had possibly hired the Boys to steal John Henry's cattle, and he also wasted no opportunity to threaten and insult John Henry.

All this meant that John Henry knew he needed armed support, both at his general store and on his ranch, and the Kid worked on the latter. He was all too happy to leave the Boys behind. Even though the Kid was officially a murderer, he was a long way from being a toughened gang member. They also treated him poorly, considering him to be nothing but a child, even throwing him out of the camp at times. The Kid hadn't known where else to go; John Henry's offer must have felt like a reprieve. In reality, it would drag him far deeper into the world of death and murder.

The Kid spent a few blissful winter months working as a cowboy and guard on John Henry Tunstall's ranch, but things grew steadily worse for everyone on the Tunstall side of the growing feud. Alexander McSween was jailed for embezzlement charges that were almost certainly false. Later, Dolan threatened John Henry directly, even going as far as drawing his pistol.

John Henry appears to have taken these threats seriously, although not seriously enough to get out of the business. The men who worked for him were always armed; in fact, he gave the Kid a Winchester rifle. The Kid appears to have loved the structure and stability that his life as John Henry's cowboy gave him. He worked with men who, while tough, were more interested in business than crime. They also took an instant liking to the charming young boy, and they appear to have readily accepted him despite his involvement with the Boys. The foreman, Dick Brewer, became someone that the Kid looked up to and admired.

But just as it seemed that the Kid might be on a more reputable path, disaster struck. A court order was issued to John Henry, claiming that the cattle on his ranch had to be seized in connection with McSween's ongoing court battle to prove his innocence. John Henry knew he couldn't save all of his livestock from being taken, but he had just won back his horses from Billy the Kid and the rest of the Boys, and he wasn't about to let them go once more.

Sheriff William Brady, who supported Dolan and the House, knew that John Henry wasn't going to let his horses go without a fight. He gathered a posse that included Jesse Evans—the Kid's erstwhile boss in the Boys—and sent it to John Henry's ranch on February 18th, 1878. When the posse leader, William Morton, got there, the horses and John Henry were gone. He had driven them toward Lincoln, hoping to hide them in a nearby canyon.

John Henry was riding at the head of his herd, accompanied by Dick Brewer and Deputy US Marshal Robert Widenmann. The Kid and another ranch hand, John Middleton, were riding along behind the herd, doing what was called "riding drag." Their job was to keep the horses moving smartly along as they fled from the posse. It was unpleasant work, hot and dusty and frightening, but the Kid was doing his best.

A sudden flutter of wings startled some of the horses. When the Kid looked up, he saw some wild turkeys fluttering among the sagebrush nearby. Wild turkeys were good eating, and they were much prized in the Old West. Anticipating that they might overnight out in the desert, the two men riding with John Henry rode after the turkeys, wanting to shoot them for dinner.

That was when the Kid spotted it: dust rising like a rooster's tail on the horizon. It was a familiar pattern, one that he had seen all too often. He knew that the dust had been kicked up by the hooves of galloping horses. The posse was coming, and the Kid panicked.

John Middleton set spurs to his horse, riding to warn John Henry. The Kid rode toward Dick and Robert, trying wildly to get their attention. It was too late. The posse was upon them. John Henry was alone. There was an awful crack, and the Kid remembered the way the sound rang through the saloon in Bonita, felt once again the slick warmth of Windy Cahill's blood. Only this time, the Kid was not the killer. Jesse Evans was, and he had shot John Henry in the head at point-blank range with no warning. Bill Morton had also shot John Henry, likely in the chest.

John Henry fell out of the saddle, dead, and with him fell the Kid's last hope of living a normal life. His world was shattered once again.

Seeking retribution, the following day, Dick and the Kid approached the local justice of the peace and testified to him that John Henry's killing had been cold-blooded murder. The justice of the peace, already disgruntled with the fact that Sheriff Brady had composed almost his entire posse from known outlaws, was quick to make them both his deputies and told them to go and arrest Jesse Evans and the other Boys who had been in the posse. But when Dick and the Kid approached the building where the posse was hiding with Sheriff Brady, the sheriff took the law into his own hands. He captured the two grieving men, ostensibly arresting them. They were released two days later, on February 22nd, 1878, when Marshal Widenmann arrested Brady's jailers and set Dick and the Kid free.

Even though the Kid had only known John Henry for a matter of months, he was deeply bereaved after the rancher's death, and he struggled to come to terms with what he had lost. In the harsh language of the frontier, he could think of only one answer to grief: revenge.

Dick Brewer was thinking along the same lines, and seeing that the local government was either turning a blind eye or siding with Sheriff Brady, he decided that the only thing he could do was to form a group of vigilantes in a bid to overthrow the House, support Alexander McSween, and avenge John Henry Tunstall's tragic young death. The Kid, who was approaching nineteen, was one of the first men to join the group, which became known as the Lincoln County Regulators.

The Regulators were quick to spring into action. On March 9th, 1878, Dick, the Kid, and others bloodied their hands as Regulators for the first time. They captured two of the men who had been involved in John Henry's killing: Frank Baker and, most importantly, Bill Morton, the leader of Sheriff Brady's posse and one of the men who had killed John Henry. Later, they would say that Baker and Morton were killed when they fought back in an attempt to escape the Regulators' clutches. However, it's far more likely that the two men were executed. The Regulators had decided that they were a law unto themselves. Frontier justice was brutally served, and the Kid, warped by grief, was all for it.

For several weeks, the Regulators were less active, and it almost seemed as though the Lincoln County War might be over. Then they struck again on April 1st, 1878, this time even more violently. Sheriff Brady and two of his cronies, George Hindman and Bill Matthews, were walking down Lincoln's main street when Regulators suddenly erupted from all around them in a devastating ambush. The Kid was focused on one thing: vengeance. While the other Regulators wanted to take down Sheriff Brady, as he was perceived as the leader of the House's supporters, the Kid blamed Bill Matthews most for John Henry's death. He fired at him wildly, and Matthews ducked under cover. It was evident now that the Kid was no longer the frightened boy who had accidentally shot Windy Cahill. He was ready to kill.

Meanwhile, Dick and the others killed Hindman and Brady. The bullets went quiet, and the Kid noticed something lying on the ground beside Brady: the Winchester rifle that John Henry had given him. He hurried over to the dead man to retrieve his gun, and Bill Matthews appeared from behind cover and fired. The bullet slashed through the Kid's hip with blinding pain. It was frightening and excruciating, but when the smoke had cleared, his friends assured him that he was all right—the wound was merely a graze.

So it was that the Kid, still nursing the minor injury, was with Dick, John Middleton, and the other Regulators three days later when they all trooped over to a little restaurant in a tiny nearby village known as Blazer's Mill. It consisted of little more than a post office, a tiny store, a mill, and a few houses, but it had hot food. The Regulators were all fugitives now, having murdered Brady and Hindman, and they had fled the Lincoln area to lie low in Blazer's Mill. But they found far more than a peaceful meal there.

Andrew "Buckshot" Roberts was also headed for Blazer's Mill on that tragic day. A grizzled old veteran of the West, Buckshot was a buffalo hunter and rancher. He had been a supporter of the House at one point, but after John Henry's death, he foresaw trouble. In fact, he had just sold his ranch in the area and came to Blazer's Mill to get payment from the buyer. Instead, he found a deadly battle.

When Buckshot arrived, the Regulators quickly realized that this was an opportunity to take down one of their enemies. One of them went outside to talk with Buckshot in a bid to get him to surrender. Knowing how Baker and Morton had died, Buckshot refused. Minutes later, Dick sent three of his men outside to dispose of the old hunter.

Outnumbered though he was, Buckshot proved to be a deadly opponent in a gunfight. No sooner had the armed men walked out of the restaurant than Buckshot was pouring bullets at them, wounding three men in quick succession. One of them, Charlie Bowdre, managed to get off a shot and wounded Buckshot badly in the chest, but the old cowboy still had life in him and went on shooting until his gun ran empty.

The Kid had been staying under cover in the restaurant while the bullets flew, but when he heard the metallic click of an empty weapon, he made his move. Rushing out of the restaurant, he charged at the bleeding and unarmed Buckshot. Wounded Regulators lay everywhere; John Middleton, who had been riding alongside the Kid the day John Henry died, was badly injured and bleeding from his chest. Perhaps it was seeing John that made the Kid hesitate to use his regained Winchester. Either way, before he could attack, Buckshot reversed the pistol in his hand and dealt a ringing blow to the Kid's temple. For Billy the Kid, everything went black.

He awoke to a devastating scene. The gunfight had been a brutal one. Wounded though he was, Buckshot crawled into a nearby house. The other Regulators all rushed to care for their wounded, but Dick Brewer was irate and blinded with grief and vengeance. He recklessly put himself in Buckshot's line of fire, and the old hunter shot him dead. Buckshot himself died shortly afterward.

This brutal killing was by no means the end of the Lincoln County War. It would grow even bloodier as time went on, and with every tragic attack and killing, the Kid only grew more desensitized to the violence, more accustomed to fighting and to murder.

The Regulators lay low for a few weeks after the death of Buckshot Roberts, but on April 29th, a new sheriff came to town to replace the murdered Brady: Sheriff George Peppin. Peppin was decidedly pro-House, and he was determined not to bring justice to Lincoln but to wipe out the Regulators. He quickly allied with Jesse Evans, and the two of them attacked and killed two Regulators on a local ranch. The Regulators realized that fighting once more was inevitable, and they prepared for battle, many of them gathering in Lincoln at Alexander McSween's house.

With Dick and John Henry both dead, Alexander McSween—whom the Kid knew as "Alex"—was the only leader that the Regulators had left. Fearing for Alex's life, George Coe, a Regulator who had his trigger finger shot off in the fight with Buckshot, decided to sit up on Alex's roof and defend his home. From this position, he famously shot and wounded one of the House's men at 350 yards.

The Kid himself next saw action on May 15th. With a group of Regulators, led by a sheriff's deputy who was on their side, he tracked, ambushed, and murdered one of the House's men.

By this point, it was clear to Alex that an all-out battle was brewing, and the Regulators' ranks had been badly thinned by the fighting. He left Lincoln in search of reinforcements, returning in mid-July 1878, accompanied by forty-one men.

Alex's return was a rallying call for the rest of the Regulators. They knew that they were going to have to take a stand, and they hastened to his side. Many of them were scattered around town in various hotels and homes, but ten stayed at Alex's house, and the Kid was among them. He had proven himself to be one of the most trusted Regulators, and Alex wanted him close by his side.

On July 15th, George Peppin rode into town, leading a posse alongside Jesse Evans—the Kid's nemesis. Evans had treated him brutally during his time as one of the Boys and had been involved in many gunfights since, and the Kid was ready to do battle against him. Immediately, fighting broke out. The innocent citizens of Lincoln could only lay low and hope for the best as the feud raged around them, bullets hissing and whining through the air, the crack of guns and the cries of the wounded filling the little frontier town.

The first casualty was one of Peppin's men. Shocked by the loss, Peppin briefly withdrew, realizing that the Regulators were more than he'd bargained for. He sent word to a nearby Army post at Fort Stanton, begging for help. The Army initially refused, and the battle dragged on day after day. Several Regulators fell, and so did another of Peppin's men. But the Regulators were gaining the upper hand.

That changed on July 18th. The thunder of hooves filled the air, drowning out even the gunfire, as the US Army came charging into Lincoln. Lieutenant Colonel Nathan Dudley was at the head of a troop of Buffalo Soldiers, which was the name given to this unit of African American men, so named by the Native Americans for the texture of their hair. They had come to Peppin's aid after all, and their strength and numbers made quick work of most of the Regulators. By the following day, only the handful of men who stayed at Alex's house were still fighting. The rest had all been captured.

The Kid knew that disaster was upon them, but he was determined to hold out, and Alex was in no frame of mind to surrender. They continued to defend Alex's adobe house as the US Army closed in on July 19th. Unable to get the Regulators to surrender, the Army decided to drive them out of the house by force. The next thing the Kid knew, the house was on fire. Thick smoke choked the rooms; Alex's home was engulfed in flames, and the Regulators could do nothing to stop it. Panic filled the air. In the chaos, many of the Regulators broke cover and dashed out into the street, where they fell like flies from the guns of the Army.

It wasn't a soldier but a House supporter named Robert Beckwith who rushed into the smoke and saw a figure coming toward him. Without looking, Beckwith fired, and the figure crumpled to the ground only for him to see that he had killed Alex McSween, who was unarmed. The Kid was appalled to see Alex fall. His next action came naturally; after all, killing was easy for him by now.

He raised his weapon, and he shot Robert Beckwith dead.

* * * *

It was the Kid who ultimately saved most of the Regulators that day. Rallying them in the single room that was not yet on fire, he led them out of Lincoln and to the comparative safety of the surrounding wilderness, becoming in one day both a killer and a hero. But it was a terrible, terrible moment for the Kid. He had just lost so many men who were important to him: Alex, John Henry, and Dick, just to name a few. And it was abundantly clear that, although spats would continue into the mid-1880s, the Lincoln County War was over. The Regulators had lost.

Now, the Kid found himself once again alone and desperate in a country filled with his enemies. He was swiftly indicted for the murder of Sheriff Brady, among others, and warrants were issued for his arrest.

Billy the Kid was a wanted man and an outlaw. And he would die for his crimes.

Chapter 4 – Dying Young

Illustration III: The gravestone that Billy the Kid shares with two of his friends

By the time a year had passed since John Henry's killing, the Kid had grown arrogant.

Hardened by the trauma of the Lincoln County War, the Kid had given up any hope of a normal life and had thrown himself into living as an outlaw. For him, that meant doing whatever he wanted: rustling horses, womanizing, drinking, gambling—he had thrown all thought of normality to the wind. He had escaped Lincoln with his life, after all, and with every month of freedom that passed, the Kid felt more and more invincible.

After the so-called Battle of Lincoln in July 1878, the Kid, along with several other Regulators, fled a hundred miles north to the village of Fort Sumner. Here, for months, the law failed to find him, and the Kid did as he pleased with his Regulator friends. There was one instance of violence when some of the Kid's new Mexican cronies clashed with the Mescalero Apache over the theft of some horses; an accountant who lived nearby, Morris Bernstein, rode into the chaos and was shot and killed by one of the Mexicans. Because the Kid was nearby, however, he was indicted for the murder.

Nonetheless, the Kid continued to evade the law and grow rich on the proceeds of horse theft. He even returned to Lincoln to steal horses from Fritz Ranch, the very same ranch where two Regulators had died in 1878. He sold them in Tascosa, Texas, and settled there for some time, continuing to live the outlaw life.

His bliss could not last long. Things were shifting and changing in Lincoln. A new governor had been appointed named Lew Wallace, who had served as a general during the American Civil War. Wallace was determined to whip New Mexico Territory into shape, starting with notorious Lincoln. His job was not made easy. Jesse Evans and the Boys were still rustling and causing trouble in Lincoln, and a new gang led by John Selman had taken it a step further, adding gang rape and the murder of children to Wallace's list of worries.

The Lincoln County War and its aftermath were a headache that Wallace just didn't need. Accordingly, he granted amnesty to all of the combatants in the war, except for those who already had indictments. The Kid didn't get to benefit from the amnesty, but he did feel as though Wallace's action was a step toward putting the feud behind him. Knowing he couldn't escape the law, the Kid hoped to escape at least the threat of being killed by the Boys, and he wrote to Jesse Evans asking if they could parley and hopefully make peace.

In the meantime, Alex McSween's widow, Susan, was seeking justice for the senseless murder of her husband. She had approached a mild-mannered attorney named Huston Chapman to assist her. He had been representing Susan for some time, and he was in Lincoln the day that the Regulators and the Boys met, February 18th, 1878, exactly one year after John Henry's death.

Surprisingly enough, the parley managed to proceed without any violence. The Boys and the Regulators agreed to put an end to their feud. The Kid shook hands with Jesse Evans, and then in true outlaw fashion, they all proceeded to the nearby saloons and became utterly intoxicated.

While the men were sitting around the street, all in an advanced state of inebriation, Huston Chapman came walking down the main street of Lincoln, where Sheriff Brady and his deputies had been killed just months earlier. Jesse Evans immediately began to mock the attorney, asking him where he was going and telling him to dance. One of his men, an excitable youngster named Billy Campbell, joined in the mocking. James Dolan, the owner of the House, was also present, and he was also drunk.

As the mocking grew worse and Chapman continued to try to get away, the Kid realized trouble was coming. He tried to leave, but Evans pointed his pistol at him and ordered him to stay.

Chapman was growing more and more tired of this tomfoolery. Eventually, he lost his patience, realizing that he was speaking with his enemies, the very men whom he wanted to bring to justice for Alex's sake. He demanded to know if he was speaking to Dolan, and Evans responded instead, saying that he was a friend of Dolan's. At that point, unprovoked, Dolan drew his weapon. He and Billy Campbell both fired, and Chapman dropped dead.

Next, Evans ordered the Kid to draw Chapman's weapon from his holster and place it in his hand so that the sheriff would think Chapman had fired first. The Kid crept nearer to the body, but instead of doing as he was told, he bolted, just managing to escape with his life.

The tragic end to what the Kid had hoped would be a treaty had broken his heart. He knew now that there was no trusting Jesse Evans and no hope for peace. To make matters worse, he feared that he would be indicted for Chapman's murder too. On top of that, the Kid had hoped that Chapman would be able to get justice for Alex. Now, he wanted to bring Chapman's killers to justice, and he could think of just one way to do that.

The Kid wrote to Wallace shortly after Chapman's death with a staggering offer: he would testify about Chapman's murder if Wallace could guarantee his safety and treat him with lenience. Wallace was quick to agree—perhaps a little too quick. Yet, the Kid, for all his killings, still had his soulful blue eyes, his smooth baby face, and the naivete to go along with it. He trusted Wallace, and on March 21st, 1879, the Kid allowed himself to be arrested and taken to Lincoln's jailhouse.

The Kid held up his end of the deal. He testified truthfully about Chapman's murder, seeing the trial through to the end, and was then returned to the jailhouse in Lincoln. Wallace, however, had no intention of honoring his promises. He ignored the Kid completely thenceforth, and the local district attorney refused to let the Kid go.

For nearly three months, the Kid languished in jail, waiting for his freedom. By June, it had become evident to him that he was never going to be set free. He was reluctant to return to the life of a wanted fugitive, but he had been left no choice. With a heavy heart, the Kid planned yet another jailbreak, escaping on June 17th, 1879.

The Kid fled straight back to Fort Sumner, where he continued to live his outlaw life, drinking, carousing, and stealing as he pleased. He had given himself over to the reality that he was a murderer and that peace would never again be possible. Killing had become almost casual to him. This was made evident on a cold evening in January 1880 when the Kid was drinking and gambling as usual with some friends in a saloon in Fort Sumner. Joe Grant, a large, loud-mouthed man, had come into the saloon just looking for trouble. He was pushing other patrons around and spoiling for a fight, and the Kid was ready to give it to him. Grant reminded him of Windy Cahill, and what was more, it is possible that Grant was planning to kill the Kid and that someone had told him this.

The Kid went up to Grant and commented on the beautiful six-shooter pistol that the man was carrying. Looming over the scrawny figure of the Kid, who was then only twenty years old, Grant handed over the pistol with drunken laughter. The Kid realized that there were less than six bullets in the cylinder. He spun it quietly to present an empty chamber to the barrel, returned the gun to Grant, and walked away.

Minutes later, Grant pulled out his pistol and fired it at the Kid. The pistol clicked on its empty chamber, and the Kid coolly returned fire, killing Grant immediately.

It was in 1880 that the Kid also befriended a rancher near Fort Sumner named Jim Greathouse. Greathouse was a wealthy and useful ally, a fact that became abundantly obvious the following November. The Kid had just turned twenty-one and was heading into another winter of stealing horses and drinking when a local sheriff's deputy decided that it was time to bring the Kid to justice. James Carlysle gathered a posse and rode to corner the Kid and some of his friends in Fort Sumner. The Kid narrowly evaded them and rode straight for Greathouse's ranch, hoping to seek shelter with his friend. Greathouse welcomed him into his home, and when James Carlysle arrived, the rancher told Carlysle that he was being held hostage. It's unclear whether this was actually the case or whether Greathouse was simply playing along.

Either way, Carlysle boldly offered to exchange himself for Greathouse as a hostage. Not only was he trying to protect the civilian, but he also wanted the opportunity to negotiate with the Kid. Greathouse agreed, and Carlysle entered the house, starting to talk to the Kid. By this time, it was obvious to the Kid that he could trust no one, especially not a lawman. Tensions escalated within the house, and Carlysle rushed for a nearby window on the second floor, breaking it open and leaping out.

He was still alive when he hit the ground, but immediately, bullets began to fly. It would appear that Carlysle's posse panicked and began randomly shooting everything that moved. Some accounts say that they even killed Carlysle themselves; others say that the Kid leaned out of the window, looked Carlysle in the eye, and shot him dead. Either way, the Kid and his friends escaped in the chaos, but it was evident to the Kid that his time was running out. The law was drawing the noose tighter and tighter around him.

The man pulling that noose was the new sheriff of Lincoln County, Pat Garrett. Strangely enough, Garrett's varied career—from a barman to a ranch hand to the county sheriff—had actually brought him into contact with the Kid during previous years. Before the Lincoln County War, Garrett and the Kid had been drinking buddies. But now, Garrett saw the Kid as his ticket to fame. He had become the stuff of legend, a bogeyman of New Mexico. Bringing him to justice would be a highlight of any lawman's career. And Pat Garrett had just been elected a few weeks before the Greathouse incident.

It didn't take long for Garrett to learn that Fort Sumner was the Kid's favorite hideout. Just weeks after the Greathouse incident, Garrett summoned a posse of his own and rode quietly into Fort Sumner to lay a trap for the Kid. The Kid was hiding out on another ranch at the time, but Garrett craftily had a note written and sent to the Kid, telling him that the lawmen had left. Delighted to be able to return to Fort Sumner and get back to his wayward life, the Kid gathered his friends—among them Tom O'Folliard, with whom he had become very close since the Lincoln County War—and rode back into Fort Sumner. Tom was riding in the front, and the first warning the Kid had of Garrett's presence was a terrible crack of gunfire. Tom slumped dead in the saddle, and Garrett and his men erupted from behind their cover.

The Kid wheeled his horse around and rode off into the fog as quickly as he could, but Garrett was close behind. Along with his remaining friends, Billy the Kid barricaded himself in a nearby ranch house. A miserable stand-off ensued the next day, December 19th, 1880. The outlaws did their best to outlast the lawmen, but where gunfire had failed, starvation and cold succeeded. The Kid gave himself up. Garrett dragged him into Fort Sumner, where the local blacksmith fitted him with heavy iron shackles on his arms and legs. Garrett wasn't going to let him escape this time.

For some months, it appeared that Garrett had succeeded. The Kid was still struggling to escape, but the jailhouse in Santa Fe proved to be far more difficult to get out of than the many cells that the Kid had previously escaped. He tried digging through the floor and ended up chained to the wall. This time, there would be no slipping away. Attorneys had little interest in representing him; in desperation, he even wrote to Wallace, who flatly ignored him. In his eyes, seeing the Kid hang would get rid of a considerable nuisance, deal or no deal.

Late in March, the Kid was moved to nearby Mesilla, where he stood trial. Ironically, it has been debated whether the two murders for which he was tried were among the many murders he actually committed. He was tried for killing Sheriff Brady, who was killed by the other Regulators during an ambush, and Buckshot Roberts, who was killed by Charlie Bowdre. However, he was found guilty on April 15th, 1881, and was sentenced to hang on May 13th, 1881.

Before the hanging, he was moved back to Lincoln, where he was confined next to Garrett's own office in the two-story courthouse. One of his guards was Bill Matthews, the very man who had given him his first gunshot wound at the very beginning of the Lincoln County War. The Kid was kept handcuffed, chained, and under twenty-four-hour guard, and it seemed that he would live out the rest of his brief and miserable days under constant scrutiny.

Perhaps this gave Garrett a false sense of security; perhaps he felt he had already won, that the Billy the Kid debacle was over even before the Kid was hanged. Either way, he left town on a tax-collecting expedition, and the Kid was left with two guards: Bob Olinger and James Bell.

On April 28th, Olinger left the room to feed the other prisoners by taking them across the street to a nearby hotel for lunch. The Kid was allowed no such luxury, but when he asked Bell to take him to the outhouse, the guard complied. The Kid was still handcuffed and shackled, but he shuffled out of the back of the courthouse with a plan in mind. He had grown very used to the handcuffs, and he knew that they were just a little big for his tiny, boyish hands. They had been the subject of ridicule before, but they served him well now. He slipped one of them out of the cuffs, whirled around, yanked Bell's weapon from his holster, and struck him over the head with it. Bell stumbled away, panicked, and bolted. The Kid coolly shot him dead in the back.

He left the dead lawman and ran back into the courthouse, looking for an ax with which to get rid of his shackles. Instead, he came across Olinger's shotgun in one of the second-story rooms. Leaning out of the window with the shotgun, he spotted Olinger hurrying back across the street.

"Look out, old boy," he called out, "and see what you get."

Olinger looked up, and he got both barrels in the chest, killing him instantly.

The Kid escaped yet again, fleeing into the desert and dodging his execution. And while he never would face the hangman's noose, his death would nonetheless be quick and violent.

* * * *

Sheriff Garrett returned to Lincoln to find Billy the Kid gone and two of his deputies killed. In response, Wallace placed a $500 bounty on the Kid's head (about $12,000 in today's money). Garrett needed little motivation to go hunting after the Kid. His gut told him to go back to Fort Sumner, and unbelievably, that was exactly where the Kid had gone. With all of the Old West before him and so many different places to flee to, the Kid was unable to resist the pull of the village that had become his home.

Questioning several people in the town, Garrett found out that the Kid was staying with an old friend named Pete Maxwell. That evening, he went to Maxwell's home. Maxwell was shocked and frightened to see Garrett, and he quickly led him up to his own bedroom, hoping to keep him away from the Kid, who was asleep in a different room. Garrett sat down and started to interrogate Maxwell, desperate to find out where the Kid was but reluctant to be violent with the apparently innocent Maxwell. Maxwell talked in circles, trying not to tell Garrett anything, but the nervous pitch of his voice woke the Kid.

It was very dark, and when the Kid entered Maxwell's room, neither he nor Garrett recognized one another at first. Still, the Kid had heard Garrett's voice, and he knew there was a stranger inside. He drew his weapon, asking Maxwell, "Who is it? Who is it?" in Spanish.

Those would be his last words. The moment he spoke, Garrett knew his voice. He pulled out his gun and fired twice into the darkness. There was a terrible thud. The Kid had collapsed to the floor with a bullet in his chest, and he died there on that floor in a pool of his own blood.

Conclusion

The proverb that those who live by the sword die by the sword has never been so apt as when applied to the life of Henry McCarty, better known as Billy the Kid. Yet it seems as though the Kid's choices, while appalling, were often driven by awful circumstances.

Starting from the slums of New York City, the Kid's life was never easy. His father died when he was young, he lost his mother just a few years later, and his stepfather walked out on him. After that, the few friends he had that did not betray him were killed in front of him. Anytime a semblance of peace or structure came into his life, it was cruelly torn away from him.

Nonetheless, it is certain that the Kid, folk hero though he has become, was a cold-blooded killer. He may have been pressured by circumstances, but at the end of the day, he alone made the choice to pull the trigger time and time again.

Here's another book by Captivating History that you might like

Free Bonus from Captivating History (Available for a Limited time)

Hi History Lovers!

Now you have a chance to join our exclusive history list so you can get your first history ebook for free as well as discounts and a potential to get more history books for free! Simply visit the link below to join.

Captivatinghistory.com/ebook

Also, make sure to follow us on Facebook, Twitter and Youtube by searching for Captivating History.

Sources

Andrews, E. 2020, *9 Things You May Not Know About Billy the Kid*, A&E Television Networks, viewed February 2021 <https://www.history.com/news/9-things-you-may-not-know-about-billy-the-kid>

The Editors of the Encyclopedia Britannica 2020, *Billy the Kid*, Encyclopedia Britannica, viewed February 2021 <https://www.britannica.com/biography/Billy-the-Kid-American-outlaw>

Weiser, K. 2019, *Billy the Kid – Teenage Outlaw of the Southwest*, Legends of America, viewed February 2021 <https://www.britannica.com/biography/Billy-the-Kid-American-outlaw>

History.com Editors 2020, *Legendary outlaw Billy the Kid is born*, A&E Television Networks, viewed February 2021, <https://www.history.com/this-day-in-history/billy-the-kid-born>

Biography.com Editors 2019, *Billy the Kid*, A&E Television Networks, viewed February 2021, <https://www.biography.com/crime-figure/billy-the-kid>

Brothers, M. 2015, *About Billy the Kid* website, viewed February 2021, <http://www.aboutbillythekid.com/index.html>

O'Sullivan, N. 2013, *Scary Tales of New York: life in the Irish slums*, The Irish Times, viewed February 2021, <https://www.irishtimes.com/culture/scary-tales-of-new-york-life-in-the-irish-slums-1.1335816>

Hawksville, A. 2018, *Billy the Kid*, Black Horse Westerns, viewed February 2021, <https://bhwesterns.com/article/billy-the-kid/>

Smith, M. T., *Henry Clay Hooker*, Nevada Trivia, viewed February 2021, <https://nevadatrivia.com/nevada-history/henry-clay-hooker/>

History.com Editors 2020, *Billy the Kid Kills his First Man*, A&E Television Networks, viewed February 2021, <https://www.history.com/this-day-in-history/billy-the-kid-kills-his-first-man>

Simkin, J. 2020, *Lincoln County War*, Spartacus Educational, viewed February 2021, <https://spartacus-educational.com/Wwlincolnwar.htm>

Weiser-Alexander, K. 2021, *John Tunstall – Murdered in the Lincoln County War*, Legends of America, viewed February 2021, <https://www.legendsofamerica.com/john-tunstall/>

Drew, Dr. D. 2013, *John Henry Tunstall – The Man Who Started the Lincoln County War*, Cowboy Country Magazine, viewed February 2021, <https://www.cowboycountrymagazine.com/2013/02/john-henry-tunstall-the-man-who-started-the-lincoln-county-war/>

Simkin, J. 2020, *Dick Brewer*, Spartacus Educational, viewed February 2021, <https://www.cowboycountrymagazine.com/2013/02/john-henry-tunstall-the-man-who-started-the-lincoln-county-war/>

Simkin, J. 2020, *Alexander McSween*, Spartacus Educational, viewed February 2021, <https://spartacus-educational.com/WwmcsweenA.htm>

Murphy, P. 2006, *Billy the Kid and the Lincoln County War: the Irish connection*, History Ireland, viewed February 2021,

<https://www.historyireland.com/18th-19th-century-history/billy-the-kid-and-the-lincoln-county-war-the-irish-connection/>'

Dixon, M. N. 2017, *The Sad Fate of Huston Chapman*, Nicole Madalo Dixon, viewed February 2021, <http://nicolemaddalodixon.blogspot.com/2017/09/the-sad-fate-of-huston-chapman.html>

Illustrations:

Illustration I: https://commons.wikimedia.org/wiki/File:Billykid.jpg

Illustration II: By Unknown author - File:Джон Танстелл.jpg, Public Domain, https://commons.wikimedia.org/w/index.php?curid=46457963

Illustration III: https://commons.wikimedia.org/wiki/File:Billy_the_Kids-grave_texas.jpg

www.ingramcontent.com/pod-product-compliance
Lightning Source LLC
LaVergne TN
LVHW042001060526
838200LV00041B/1816